Published by Flowerpublishing
©2018 Afshin Effati
ISBN 978-1-927914-86-1
All rights reserved. No part of this book may be reproduced, stored in a retrieval system or transmitted in any form or by any means without the prior written permission of the publisher, except by a reviewer who may quote brief passages in a review to be printed in a newspaper, magazine or journal

I0141782

Flowerpublishing
www.flowerpublish.com
Montreal Canada

I'm sincerely grateful to Flowerpublishing, especially Maryann Hayatian for supporting and encouraging me to publish this book

Cello Riffing

Afshin Effati

This idea is simply beautiful, fascinating and exciting:
Playing Riff and rock music with the cello
The idea is practically inspired by the same world of classical music and earns respect with the words of greed, honesty and earnestness. At classical music we learn to get real strong feelings, we have to have something to compare with it.
Thus, doing something nice and hard is even harder than what it looks like. If it is just hard, it is no longer that hard. For this reason, it seems that there is no room to criticize this idea. However, there are many classical musicians not understanding this type of music, which is why they do not understand output and the purpose

Honestly, if we even create a slight change in the feelings of the next generation of classical instrumentalists, especially the cello, it is the only one needed to play an instrument well and beautifully. The goal is to show that we can do whatever we want with the instruments. If we just want, if we are open minded and let ourselves do it. As a musician, I think it is always nice and beautiful to create something new. Sometimes it is hard because we have always played the others' pieces, especially since some contemporary composers do not make specific pieces for the audience. To perform this style, one should naturally change in the technique of playing so that it can be presented with this style. Given that in this type of music, it should often be very fast, heavy and strong, the use of black hair bows more common in double bass, as well as double bass rosin, are more effective and faster, because It makes a huge grip on the string. The beauty of the output sound of this type of bow can be further understood by playing solo melodies. To play heavy and base Riffs, should be used this kind of bow because; otherwise, using usual bow of the cello, white hair and its rosin cannot be accented, what is needed at the very beginning.

Example 1 -- The normal bow hold....

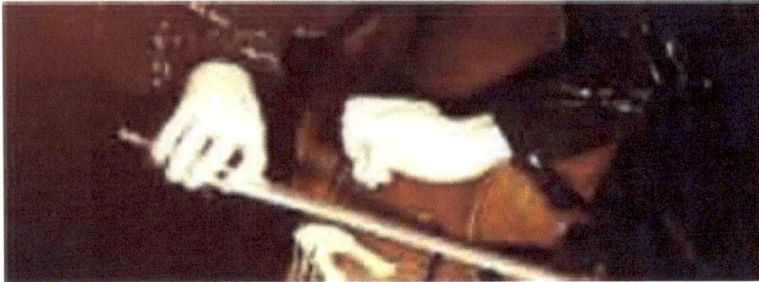

Example 2 -- and the alternative bow hold....

If you hold the bow like Example 1, you can't use that much force. If you put it like Example 2 you have more weight and more power in your hand.

Same thing for instance what Rostropovich does when he plays Shostakovich concerts. Sometimes the fingers 3 and 4 get away from the fingerboard, and the wrist plays a key role in performing those heavy speed parts and Riffs. Example 1 is a great example for the solos and all the technique the fingers should be used. Concerning the left-hand technique, other than the single note, the fifth intervals are also very useful, in which case two strings are taken together with the folding fingers on the fingerboard.

This is something not always used in classical music. The following images well show the shape of the left fingers in this form.

To create distortions sounds and ornaments in riffs, other than acoustic techniques such as fast and ranged vibrations like that of like that of glissando, known as (Morocco Vibrato) and the harmonic notes, one can use a good electrical equipment, which is a very important feature in this style. In doing so, the use of electric cello is not advisable as the microphone is only embedded under one foot of the bridge not on both sides and it is on the A string side, so the A string sound is quite good, but the C and G are weak, there is no power anymore. In any case, it's much greater to play with normal classical instruments and to get the real contrast of the huge sound to those classical cellos...those old instruments. With a normal cello it's resonating, when you play, you can feel that. With an electric cello you can't, it's not resonating. Just like a dead body. In the following image, one can easily see how to install the pickup and other related electrical equipment.

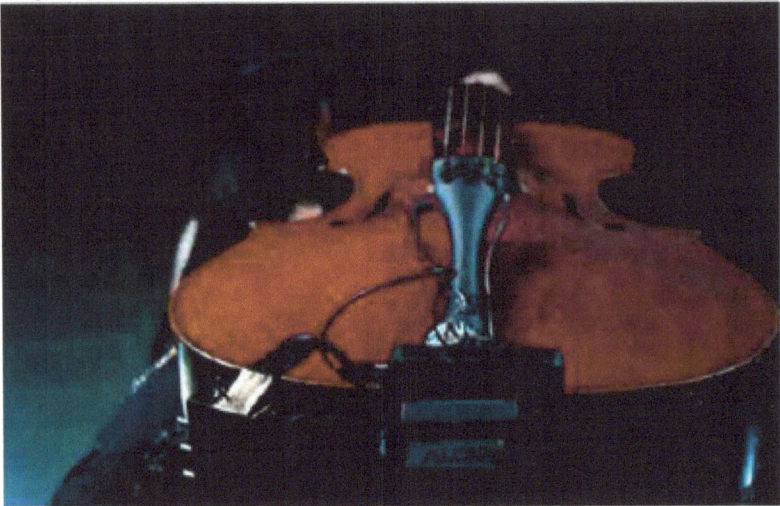

We look at some of the available equipment for this purpose.

- Barcus-Berry and Schertler pickups

- BB 3000A and StatPre preamps

- Line 6 Bass Pod

- EBS Multidrive pedal

- EBS Octabass pedal

- MXR 10-band EQ

- Peavey 6505+ amp (listed on Peavey site)

- G-Labs GSC-3, MGC-6, M3S, PB-1, AUX Bank Up/Down with midi in (G-Labs site)

The best way to practice the fifth intervals and their fingerings is scaling. They can be used for octave double chords double stops for this purpose, the following examples are helpful.

2 NOTE CHORDS

2 NOTE NON-ADJACENT

The first pattern of double note practice is the chromatic scale on C and G strings, which also goes for double notes of G, D, and D- A and is a fantastic practice. The second pattern is the practice of non-adjacent double notes, where thumb technique can be used for octave.

Major scales plain with their fifth intervals

Major scales-plain in 5ths

Minor scales plain with their fifth intervals

Minor scales-plain in 5ths

To simplify the type of practicing the scales above can first be started by practicing the simple the fingers shifting on the two strings without removing them and moving them over to the fingerboard. Note the following:

Shifting

Another method of doing this is to split the double to high and low notes, which is to begin with playing the above notes, or the same as melody, to the end and doing the same for the lower notes. Then repeat the same thing by placing each finger on two strings while playing a single note. Now in the third practice, we start playing two notes, but in order from low down to high up note and then from high up to low down note, and then synchronize, and vice versa. Finally, with the imagination the sound of each note, we start to play two notes simultaneously. We note that it is very important that this exercise to be done initially infinitely slow, regardless of rhythm or pattern to give the ear and fingers an opportunity to find the right place with proper tone and song. The best way to find out the right way of bowing in double notes practicing is starting with the open strings, as regards that they are tune in fifth interval to one another.

The following technique is also available for bowing heavy riffs:

That means instead of bowing at the same time on the two strings, alternately and fast we bow first on the up string or the melody note, and then on the bottom string, or probably in some cases, when the speed is too high, it is just a hint and knock.

Violoncello 4

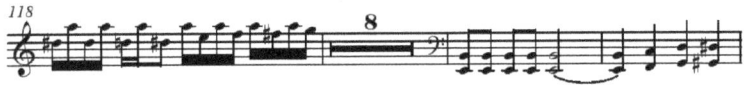

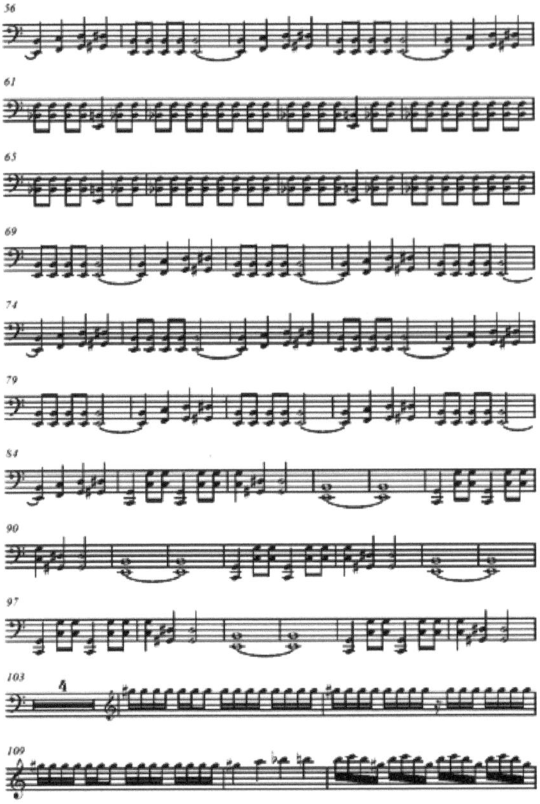
56
61
65
69
74
79
84
90
97
103
4
109

Refuse Resist

Violoncello 4

Refuse Resist

lo 4

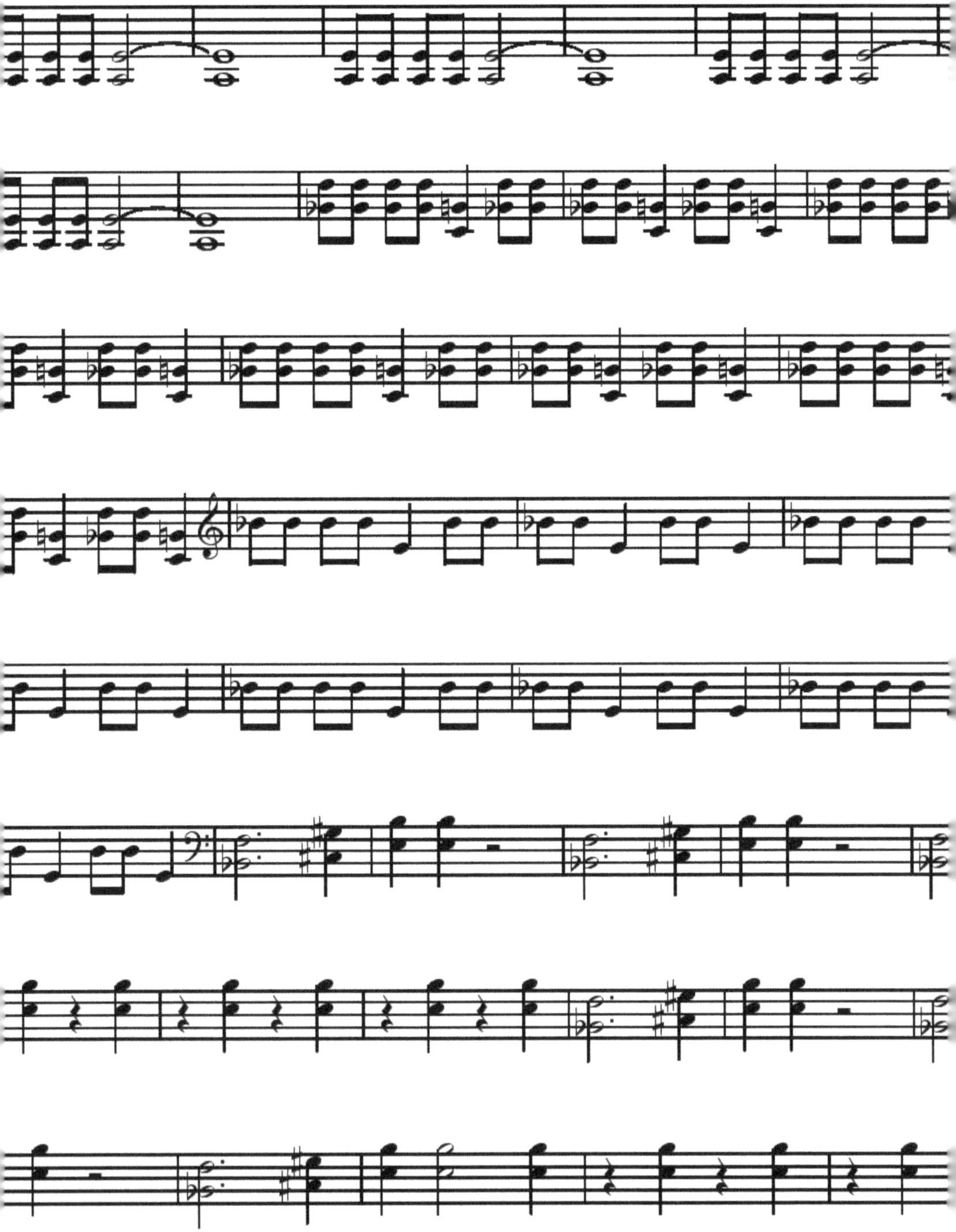

Cello 3

Faraway

Apocalyptica

2

[Title]

Bittersweet for 4 Cellos

Cello 4

Apocalyptica

[Title]

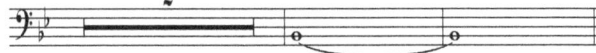

www.ingramcontent.com/pod-product-compliance
Lightning Source LLC
Chambersburg PA
CBHW041756050426

42443CB00023B/13

9781927914861